Water in the house

Sue Palmer and Ron Murphy

This book tells you how fresh water is brought to
most homes, and how dirty water is taken away.
It is also about the plumbing inside a house.
You do not have to read the book from beginning to end.
You can just turn to the pages that interest you.

Contents

Water in the house

Most people in Britain have water in the house. We turn on the tap and out comes the water.

Dirty water goes away down the plughole.

Two hundred years ago most houses
in Britain did not have taps so people had to
walk to collect water.

In those days houses did not have
plugholes or drains, so people just threw
away their dirty water outside the houses.

In the past people had to fetch their water from a pump
or a well.

Where does the water come from?

Water for our houses comes from rivers or reservoirs. These collect rain water.

This lake is called a reservoir. It collects water for us to use.

The water is cleaned at the pumping station.

The rain water is cleaned.
Then it is pumped to our homes through big pipes called water mains.

Long underground pipes called water mains bring clean water to our homes.

Water from the main pipe

A pipe from the water main
brings fresh water into the house.
The pipe leads to the kitchen taps first.
Then it takes water to a
storage tank in the roof.

The water that goes to the kitchen taps
comes straight from the mains so it should
be safe to drink.

Water from other taps in the house
may not be so fresh.
It may have been lying in the
storage tank for a long time.

hot water
cylinder

Key

cold water pipe
mains water pipe
hot water pipe

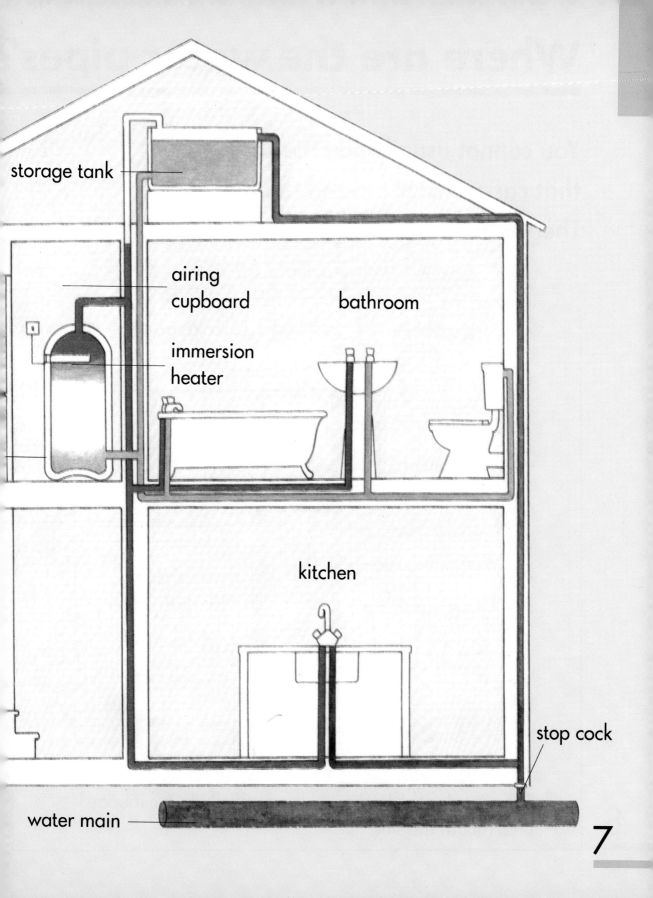

storage tank

airing cupboard

immersion heater

bathroom

kitchen

stop cock

water main

7

Where are the water pipes?

You cannot usually see the pipes
that carry water around the house.
They are hidden away.

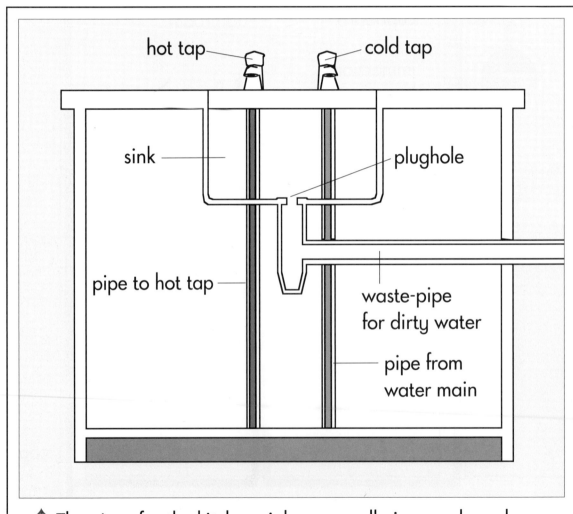

The pipes for the kitchen sink are usually in a cupboard underneath the sink.

Water pipes are hidden all over the house –
inside walls, under the floorboards and in cupboards.
The pipes and other waterworks in a house
are called the plumbing.

The person who puts new pipes and waterworks
into a house is called the plumber.
Plumbers also fix the plumbing when it goes wrong.

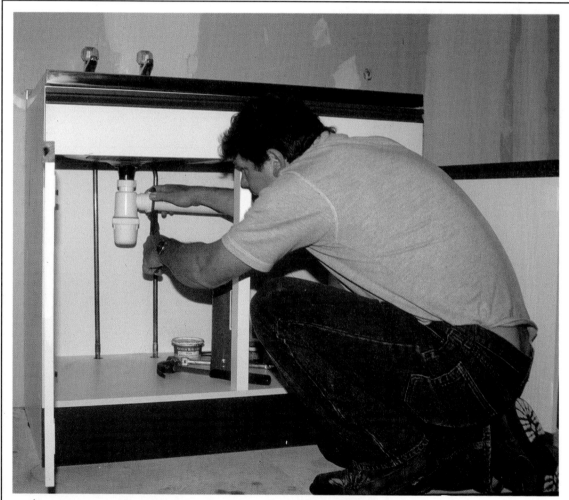

⬆ If anything goes wrong with the water pipes,
a plumber can fix it.

Where does the bath water come from?

Bath water comes from the storage tank.
There is a pipe from the tank to the bath tap.
This pipe is full of water.

When you turn the tap on,
you let the water out of the pipe.

When you turn the bath taps on,
water flows into the bath.
This water comes from the storage tank.
Some of the water goes through a heater
on the way to the hot tap.

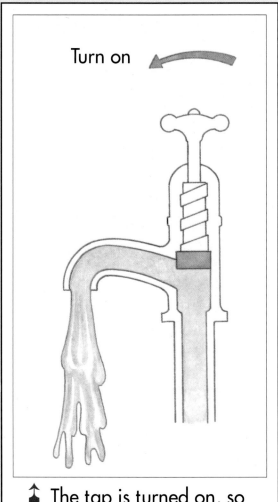

Turn on

The tap is turned on, so
the water flows out.

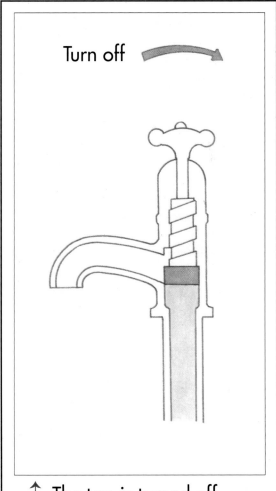

Turn off

The tap is turned off,
so the water cannot flow.

How do we get hot and cold bath water?

⬆ Be careful! Sometimes the water is very hot indeed.

The water for the cold tap in the bathroom comes straight from the storage tank to the bath.

The water for the hot tap goes through a water heater first, to get warmed up.

Different houses have different ways of warming
the hot water. In some houses the water is heated
by an electric immersion heater.

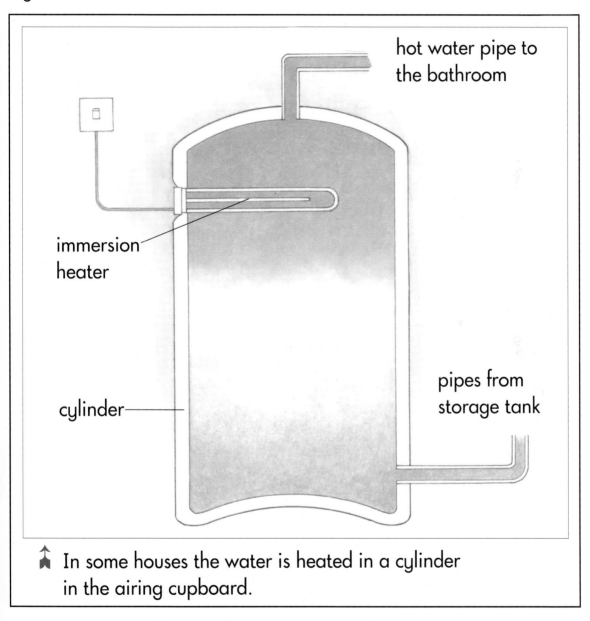

hot water pipe to
the bathroom

immersion
heater

pipes from
storage tank

cylinder

In some houses the water is heated in a cylinder
in the airing cupboard.

The heater is inside a cylinder. This cylinder is kept
full of water from the storage tank.

When you switch the heater on, it heats up the
water in the cylinder.

Where does the bath water go?

When you take the plug out of the bath the water runs down the hole into a waste-pipe. This takes the water to a main drain.
The main drain is under the house.

The waste-pipe is hidden under the plughole. ➤➤

There are waste-pipes which take dirty water away from the sink, washbasin, shower and everything else that uses water in a house. These waste-pipes carry all the dirty water into the main drain.

The waste-pipes in a house are hidden so we cannot see them.

⬆ You would have to dig a hole to see the drainpipe.

What happens when we flush the toilet?

When you flush the toilet, water rushes into the toilet pan. The water pushes the smelly waste in the pan away. It goes down a special waste-pipe to the main drain.

A toilet has its own water tank called a cistern.
The cistern is filled with water from the storage tank.

When you flush the toilet, all the water in the
cistern empties out into the toilet pan.
You can hear it filling up again straight away.

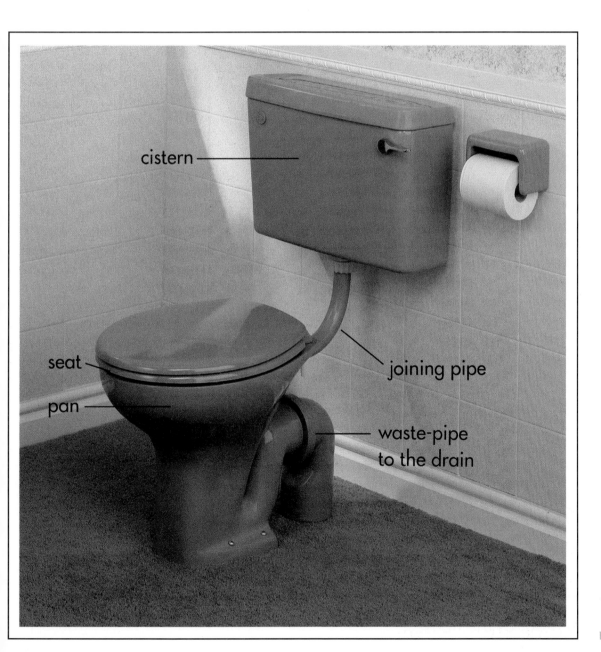

cistern

seat

pan

joining pipe

waste-pipe
to the drain

Drains and smells

Drains are pipes that take the dirty water away from houses.

On the way through the waste-pipes, the smelly waste from the toilet meets up with all the other dirty water. All this dirty water helps to wash the smelly waste through the drains and out of the house.

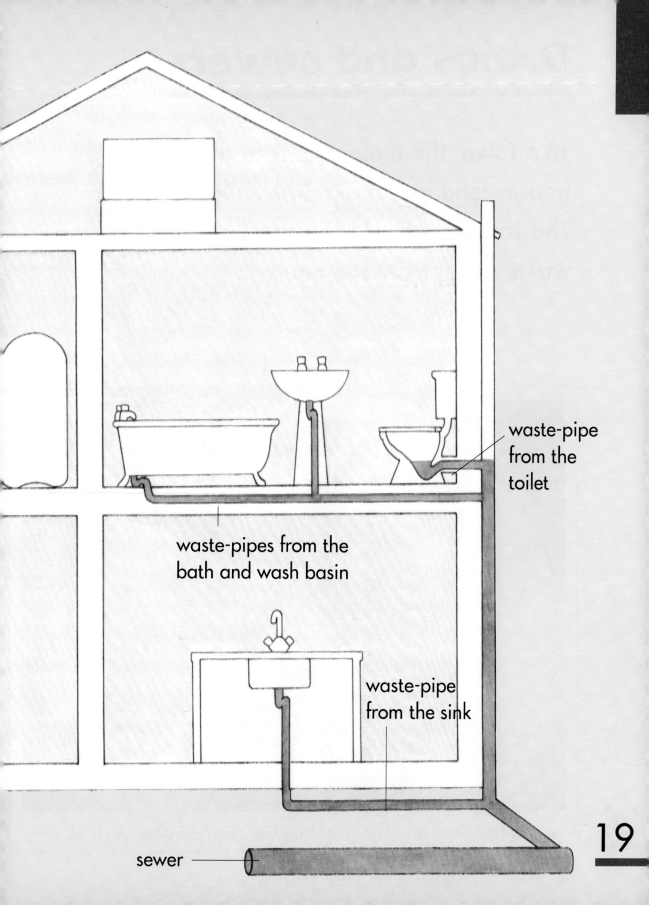

waste-pipe
from the
toilet

waste-pipes from the
bath and wash basin

waste-pipe
from the sink

sewer

19

Drains and sewers

In a town, the main drains from all the houses lead into a big pipe called a sewer. This takes all the dirty water and smelly waste away from the houses.

⬆ Some sewers are so big that people can go inside to check them.

Dirty water carries germs, so drains and sewers are important for our health. They keep the dirty water away from people and houses.

⬆ Long ago, people just threw their waste water into the street.

In the past, people often caught dangerous illnesses because they did not have proper drains and sewers.

Water workers

Water in the house is not free.
We have to pay for it.

It takes a lot of people to look after the reservoirs, pumping stations, water mains and sewers.
These people work for the water company.
We all have to pay the water company for the water we use.

↑ Sometimes a water main bursts and water workers have to fix it.

Glossary of words used in this book

Airing cupboard   An airing cupboard is a warm dry place where clothes and sheets can be stored.

Cylinder   A cylinder is a long round shape like a tube.

Drain   A drain is a pipe that takes dirty water away.

Pumping station   A pumping station is where rain water is cleaned and then pushed along the mains pipe to houses.

Reservoir   A reservoir is a lake made for storing water.

Roof space   A roof space is the gap between the upstairs ceiling of a house and the roof.

Sewer   A sewer is a drain that carries the waste water away from a house.

Stop cock   A stop cock is a tap for turning the mains water on or off.

Storage tank   A storage tank is a large container used for storing water.

Water mains   A water main is a pipe that carries fresh water to houses.

Waste   Waste is something you do not need any more. People's bodies make waste and it goes down the toilet.

Index

a b c d e f g h i j k l m n o p q r s t u v w x y z
A B C D E F G H I J K L M N O P Q R S T U V W X Y Z